MOM'S LIFE MANDALA COLORING BOOK

CRYSTAL
COLORING BOOKS

ISBN-13: 978-1986244336
ISBN-10: 1986244334

I’m
not a bad
Mom
I’m not a bad
Mom...
I’m a good mom
having a bad
day

Why is it
when I speak no
one ever
listens!!

It's
not yelling
it's
motivational
speaking

Today
was tough
but
you rocked
it!

If
being a Mom
was easy
Fathers would
do it

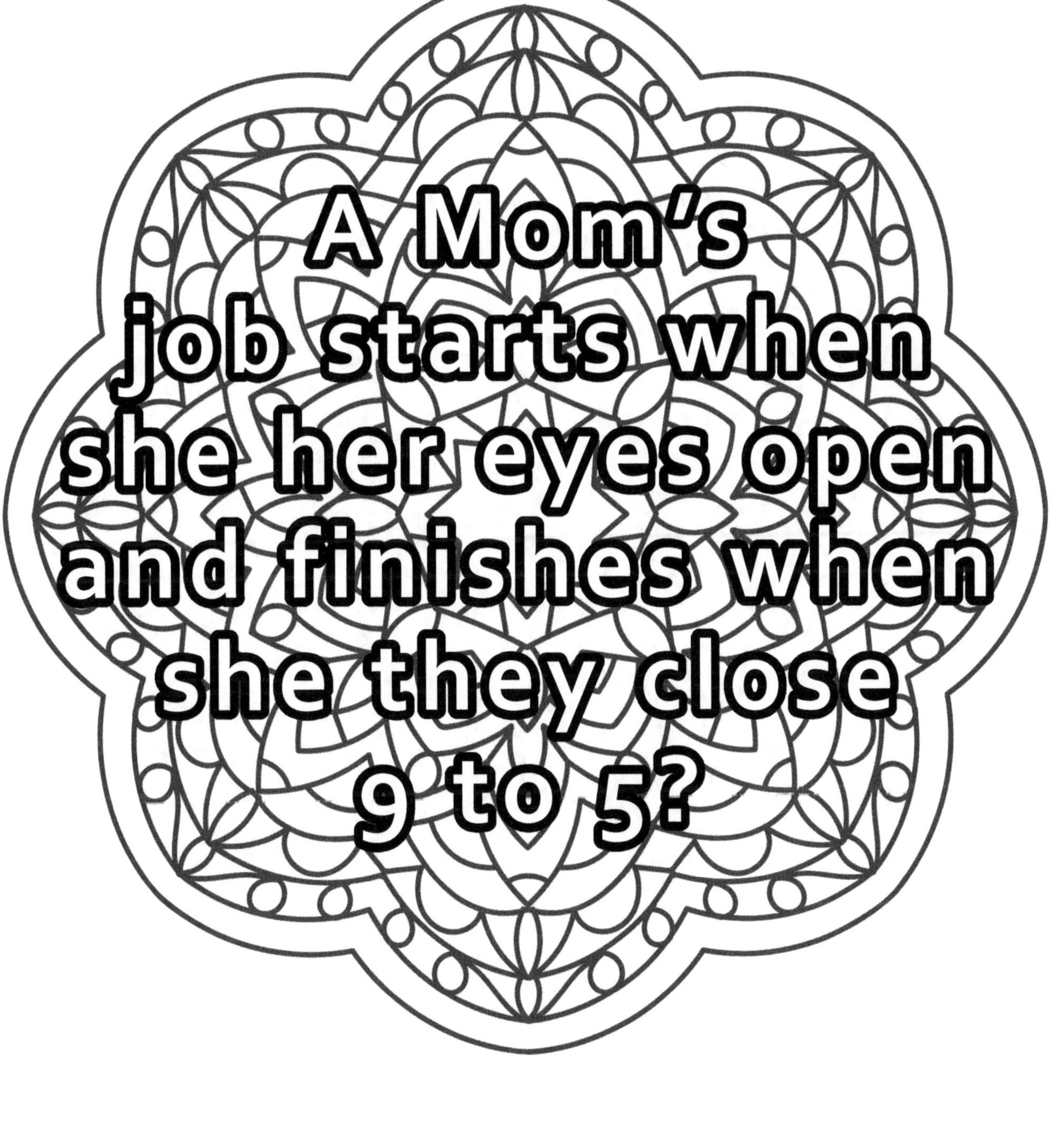
A Mom’s
job starts when
she her eyes open
and finishes when
she they close
9 to 5?

Wing
it
drink
Coffee
and pretend you
know what you
are doing

Take
one day
at a time
and
enjoy the
journey

Before
I had children
I showered
Every day

Nurse
Chef
Cleaner
Councelor
Maid
Chauffeur

The
highlight of the
day ...
enjoying a trip
to the bathroom
alone

If
you are not
tired
you are doing
it
wrong

No one
can take the
place of
a Mom

Nothing
beats being a
Mom

A Mom...
one person
that does
the work of
twenty

Happy
Stressed
But
Very
Blessed

A
Mom's Life
Is
The Best
Life

Because
I
said
so!
Mom knows best

I
am my Mom's
daughter

My
daughter will
be late for school
because...
she can put her
own shoes
on

COLOR TEST PAGE

www.ingramcontent.com/pod-product-compliance
Lightning Source LLC
Chambersburg PA
CBHW062127220526
45471CB00010B/3909
* 9 7 8 1 9 8 6 2 4 4 3 3 6 *